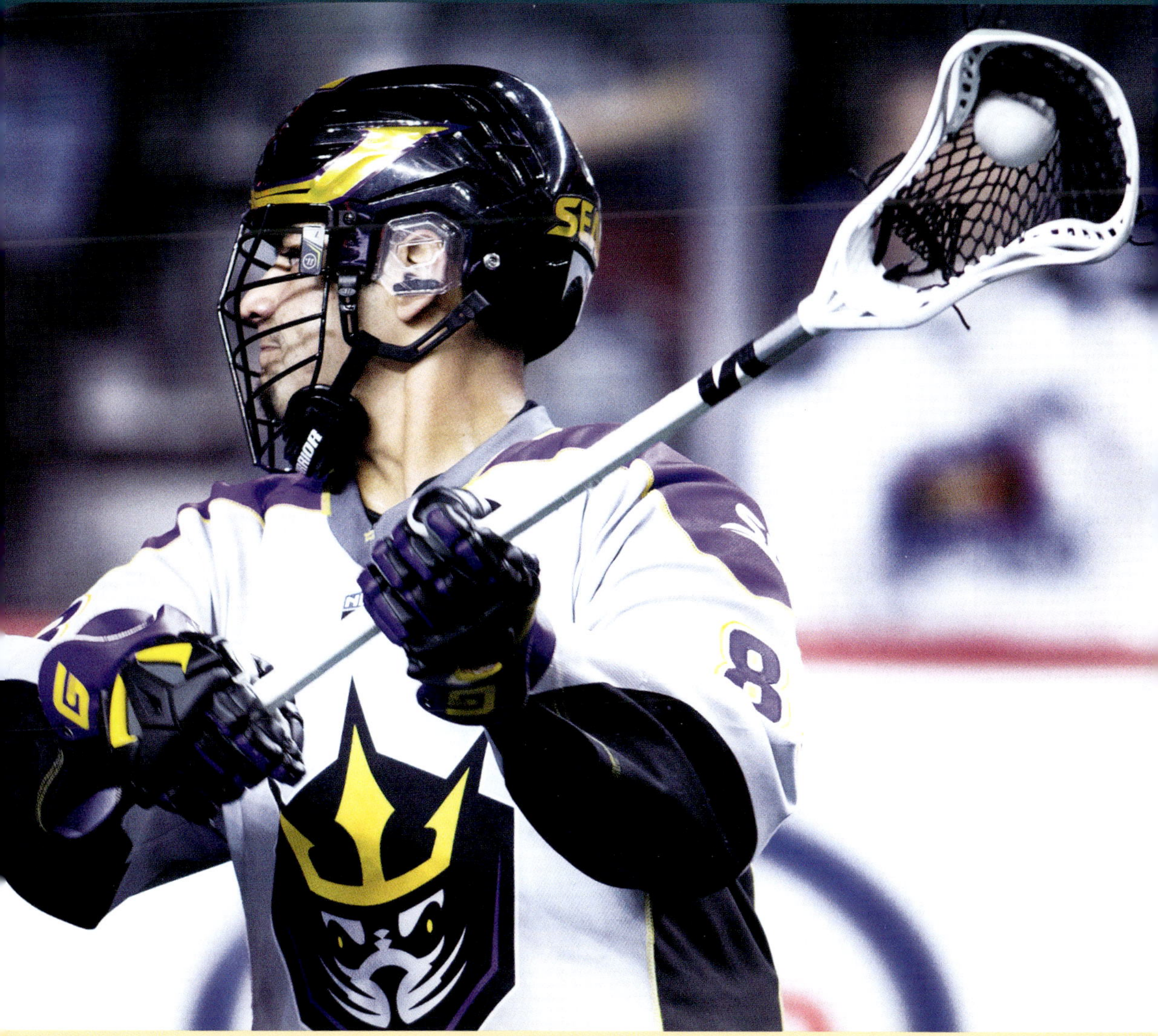

WHAT IT TAKES TO BE A PRO
LACROSSE PLAYER

by Kaitlyn Duling

www.12StoryLibrary.com

Copyright © 2020 by 12-Story Library, Mankato, MN 56002. All rights reserved. No part of this book may be reproduced or utilized in any form or by any means without written permission from the publisher.

12-Story Library is an imprint of Bookstaves.

Photographs ©: Larry MacDougal/Associated Press, cover, 1; Bill Brine/CC2.0, 4; Sparky646/CC4.0, 5; Just Life/Shutterstock.com, 6; Randy Litzinger/Icon Sportswire/Associated Press, 7; PD, 8; PD, 9; Major League Lacrosse/PD, 10; Premier Lacrosse League/PD, 10; JamesTeterenko/PD, 11; National Lacrosse League/PD, 11; Aspen Photo/Shutterstock.com, 12; c w/CC2.0, 13; Jim Larrison/CC2.0, 14; weervector/Shutterstock.com, 15; James Marvin Phelps/Shutterstock.com, 16; jpglive2/CC2.0, 17; Winslow Townson/Associated Press, 18; dcJohn/CC2.0, 19; WoodysPhotos/Shutterstock.com, 20; Larry MacDougal/Associated Press, 21; James A Boardman/Shutterstock.com, 22; DMighton/CC4.0, 23; Tom Nappi/CC2.0, 24; Au Kirk/CC2.0, 25; Pledge it/YouTube.com, 26; Andrew Schneider/US Navy, 27; Saquan Stimpson/CC2.0, 28; Schaafb32/Shutterstock.com, 29

ISBN
9781632357632 (hardcover)
9781632358721 (paperback)
9781645820468 (ebook)

Library of Congress Control Number: 2019938636

Printed in the United States of America
July 2019

About the Cover
NLL player Austin Staats makes a pass for the San Diego Seals in 2018.

Access free, up-to-date content on this topic plus a full digital version of this book. Scan the QR code on page 31 or use your school's login at 12StoryLibrary.com.

Table of Contents

Life as a Lacrosse Pro: The Real Story 4

A Day in the Life 6

A Brief History of the Game 8

One Game, Three Leagues 10

What about Women? 12

Community, School, and Beyond 14

Playing at the College Level 16

A Chance at the Pros 18

Train Like a Pro 20

Safety and Equipment 22

Play Like a Champion 24

Giving Back 26

Fun Facts about Lacrosse 28

Glossary 30

Read More 31

Index 32

About the Author 32

1

Life as a Lacrosse Pro: The Real Story

Lacrosse (LAX) has long been known as the fastest game on two feet. This fiery, high-speed game is exciting to watch and to play. Some enjoy the sport so much they play in college. After college, there are a few pro options. But they aren't fancy. The pros don't make huge salaries. They don't board team planes to fly from game to game. In fact, life as a pro lacrosse player can be pretty, well, normal. At times, it can even be hard.

There are several pro lacrosse leagues in the United States. Attacker Kevin Rice used to play for the Atlanta Blaze, a Major League Lacrosse (MLL) team. At the time, Rice lived in New York. He flew to Georgia every weekend for games. Now Rice plays in the new Premier Lacrosse League (PLL). Its teams don't have hometowns. They travel to different cities every weekend.

> Kyle Sweeney works in sports nutrition when he's not playing for the New York Lizards.

60
Nations that are members of the Federation of International Lacrosse (FIL)

- The FIL was founded in 2008. Its mission is to have LAX recognized as an Olympic sport.
- The US and Canadian national teams have both won several Men's World Championships. They are rivals who often face off against each other.
- The Australian women's team has won the Women's World Cup multiple times.

Pro LAX players don't just practice and play. They have full-time jobs, too. Goalie Adam Ghitelman is an assistant lacrosse coach at the University of Utah. When he's not coaching, he plays in the Premier Lacrosse League.

Defender Brett Schmidt plays for the Charlotte Hounds. He's also a wealth advisor. Making a living while playing pro LAX means a packed schedule. Some pros play for their home countries, too. Lacrosse is not an Olympic sport. A worldwide LAX championship is held every four years. Between games, jobs, and practices, players stay very busy.

A Day in the Life

Do pro lacrosse players live like celebrities? No, but they do get to play the sport they love. They get paid for it, too. But the low salaries, especially when compared to other pro sports, can be a challenge.

Most of the pros have day jobs. They fit in LAX training wherever they can. Midfielder Scott Ratliff trains every single day. He works out first thing in the morning. Then he takes time for coffee. Other players start their days with foam rolling. It helps their muscles recover from exercise.

On game weekends, most MLL players fly or drive in on Friday night. They practice with the team on Saturday morning. Games are played on Saturday afternoons.

Lacrosse is a sprinting game. Players run between three to five miles per game. It's important that they fuel up. The Boston Cannons usually eat a meal three hours before the game. Then they snack on fruit while they warm up.

On Sunday, everyone heads home. They start another week of work and workouts. The schedule can be exhausting.

Foam rolling helps muscles recover and improves flexibility.

3
Midfielder Kyle Harrison's age when he started playing lacrosse

- Harrison was captain of the Johns Hopkins University lacrosse team.
- After college, he joined the MLL. He also played on the national team.
- Today his life is a balancing act. Along with playing lacrosse, Harrison is president and CEO of Charm City Youth Lacrosse. This nonprofit gives kids in Baltimore a chance to play lacrosse.

BEST OF THE BEST

Most pro LAX players don't become famous. Midfielder Paul Rabil is the sport's biggest celebrity. Rabil started playing at age 12. He won two national championships in college. Then he went pro. He took home many awards and Most Valuable Player (MVP) titles. Today he heads the Premier Lacrosse League.

Paul Rabil in 2019.

3

A Brief History of the Game

Jeremy, Jerome, Miles, and Lyle Thompson are lacrosse-playing brothers. They were standout college players. Today they are pros. They have many fans. They even launched their own line of Nike gear.

The Thompson brothers don't just love the sport. As Native Americans, they are closely connected to it. Lacrosse was first played by Native people in North America. They believed it was a gift to humans and a medicine game. It was played for the enjoyment of the Creator.

English explorers and French missionaries saw the game played by Native tribes. Early settlers removed Native people from their lands and forced them to move west. The game followed. Tribes in different regions played with varied

Lacrosse was first played by Native Americans.

The Canadian Richmond Hill lacrosse team in 1885.

1805
Year when the city of La Crosse, Wisconsin, was founded

- The sport of lacrosse is woven into the early history of the United States. There are many records of settlers watching tribes play the game throughout the 1700s.
- The original name for the Wisconsin city was Prairie La Crosse.
- A sculpture of three Native American lacrosse players is found in downtown La Crosse. It is made of Cor-Ten steel. There is a fiberglass copy at the north entry to the city.

rules and equipment. French settlers named the game *la crosse*, for "crooked stick."

Lacrosse was played only by Native Americans until the mid-1800s. That's when Canadians in Montreal adopted it. They made some changes. The sport continued to grow and evolve.

LAX quickly grew popular across Canada and Europe. Today it has official rules. The official governing body of lacrosse in the United States is called US Lacrosse.

4

One Sport, Three Leagues

Most pro sports have one major league. Baseball stars play in the MLB. Football has the NFL. Lacrosse has a few different leagues.

stadiums where they play. The only exception is the Ohio Machine. Its Fortress Obetz is the first stadium in the United States that was built for lacrosse.

The oldest is Major League Lacrosse. Its first season was in 2001. It has six teams. They play in Maryland, New York, Massachusetts, Georgia, Colorado, and Texas. Midfielder Alex Woodall plays for the Atlanta Blaze. He was the top pick in the 2019 MLL Collegiate Draft. As a senior in college, Woodall won 74.2 percent of his face-offs.

In the MLL, each team plays at a set location. Most teams rent space and time from the

The Premier Lacrosse League is another pro league. It began in 2019. In the PLL, teams tour the country. There are no set stadiums. Players in the PLL make more money. They have health insurance, too. Midfielder Tom Schreiber earned many MVP titles while playing for the MLL. In 2019, he left the MLL and joined the Archers LC, a PLL team. Time will tell which league is most popular.

$8,000
Average annual salary of an MLL player

- The average salary of a PLL player is about $28,000.
- The average salary of an NBA player? $7.7 million.
- Most popular team sports, such as the NHL, NFL, and MLB, have average player salaries in the millions of dollars.

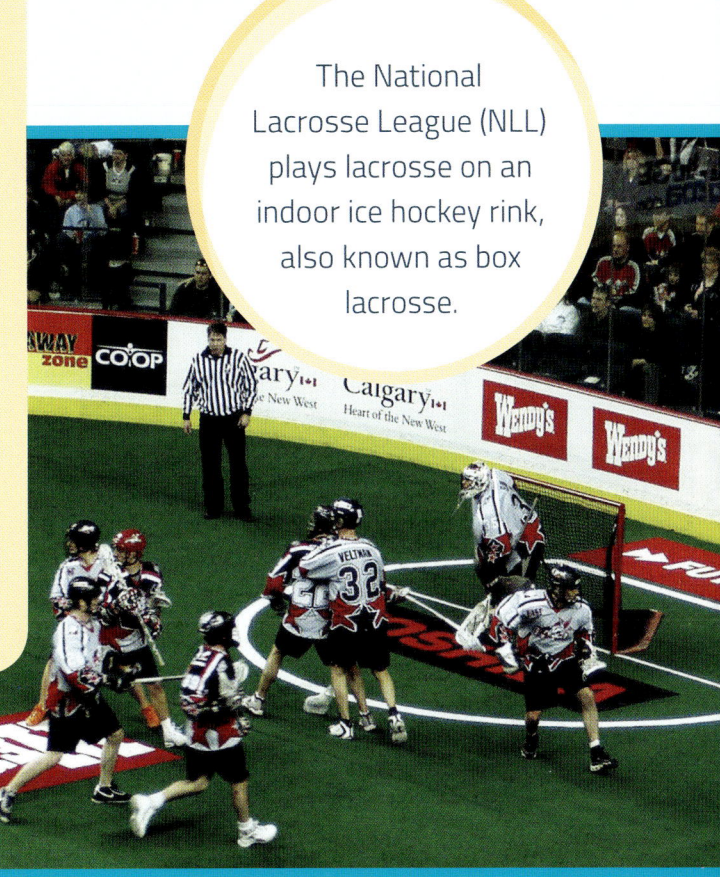

The National Lacrosse League (NLL) plays lacrosse on an indoor ice hockey rink, also known as box lacrosse.

A THIRD PRO LEAGUE

Indoor LAX is also known as box lacrosse. It has its own league. The National Lacrosse League (NLL) began in 1987. Today it has 13 teams across Canada and the United States. Box lacrosse is played on an indoor ice hockey rink. The ice is covered with fake grass. Indoor and outdoor LAX are similar. Their rules and equipment differ slightly.

5

What about Women?

Girls are playing lacrosse more than ever today.

Lacrosse isn't just a men's sport. Women and girls play, too. They are fast, strong, and competitive. More and more girls join LAX teams each year. According to the US Lacrosse annual survey, the number of girls playing the sport nearly doubled between 2007 and 2017.

The sport needs girls to join youth teams and school teams. That's how they build skills. After that, they can try out for NCAA college teams. Then they can get ready to join the

116
Number of NCAA Division I Women's Lacrosse teams in the United States

- Maryland is usually on top. In 2019, they won their 14th NCAA women's lacrosse title.
- Midfielder Jen Giles played for Maryland. Now she's a midfielder for the WPLL Pride.
- Roughly 97,000 young women play high school LAX. About 12 percent of them will play in college.

pros. Women's lacrosse has its own pro league. It's called the Women's Professional Lacrosse League. The WPLL has five teams: Brave, Command, Fight, Fire, and Pride.

The WPLL launched in 2018 with 125 players from eight different countries. Just like the men's pro players, the women don't make enough money to play full-time. Most have other jobs. They play LAX on the weekends.

The best of the best get to play on the US Women's National Team. The team competes in the world championship tournament. The United States, Australia, Canada, and England all have strong national women's teams.

SAME GAME, DIFFERENT RULES

Men's and women's LAX are slightly different. Male players are allowed to check each other. They bump and poke with their lacrosse sticks and bodies. Because of this, they wear helmets and more pads. Women's LAX has a bigger field and more players. There are 12 players per side rather than 10.

6

Community, School, and Beyond

To excel at lacrosse, most players start when they're young. The average age when children begin playing is eight and a half years. Kids as young as five often play on teams in their hometowns. Brett Garber is a third-generation lacrosse player. He's an MLL alum, too. Garber started playing in elementary school. His hobby led to high school, college, and then the pros.

Community leagues are the gateway to LAX for many players. There, kids can start at young ages. Older tweens and teens can play LAX in their middle and high schools. High school lacrosse is very popular on the East Coast. Some of the best schools for lacrosse are found in Maryland, New York, and Washington, DC.

Lacrosse-loving kids can also play on travel teams. These clubs practice multiple times a week. Then they travel to play other teams in the region. Travel teams are made up of players from different schools. The teams give players the chance to play against the very best in youth LAX.

Kids play on their hometown teams and on travel teams.

No. 1
Pick position of midfielder Myles Jones in the 2016 MLL Draft

- Today Myles Jones plays for the PLL Chaos.
- He is a two-time Tewaaraton Award finalist. The award goes to the best lacrosse player in the NCAA.
- In the summer, Jones runs LAX camps for kids and teens. Camps help players hone their skills.

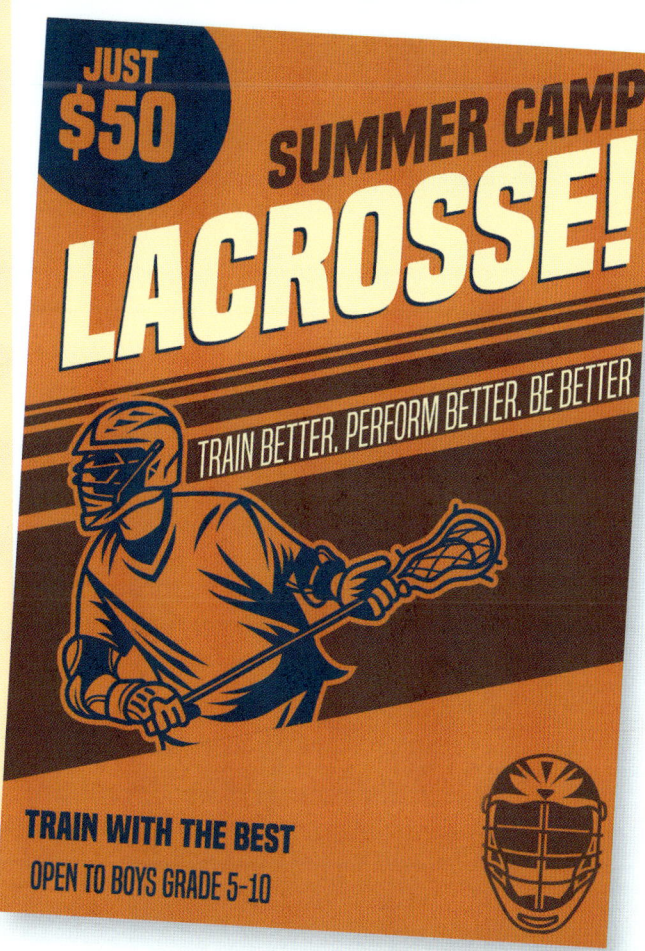

HOW MUCH DOES IT COST?

Travel lacrosse can come with a high price tag. Costs start around $1,500 for a season of travel play. That includes fees, uniforms, equipment, practice time, coach salaries, and other expenses. Sometimes costs can soar to $2,500 or more. Some nonprofit groups offer LAX at no cost to families and players.

7

Playing at the College Level

Before they go pro, many lacrosse players join college teams. The number of schools offering LAX has grown. Today there are about 900 varsity lacrosse programs at schools across the United States. Canadian colleges offer teams, too.

Some top players are recruited. They can receive valuable scholarships that help them pay for school. Attacker Pat Spencer played LAX all four years at Loyola University Maryland. It has a strong program. In his senior season, Spencer was drafted by the PLL. But Spencer is also a basketball star. He plans to put pro lacrosse on hold. He will play a year of college basketball.

Sometimes the switch from college to the pros happens in a flash. College lacrosse is lots of fun. It can be hard, too. Players face pressure to perform at a high level. They have to balance classes and practice during the week. Sometimes they take long bus rides to reach games.

Midfielder Ryan Conrad went pro just a few days after graduating college. He was a star at the University of Virginia. After helping UVA win the national championship, he got on the road. His first day with the PLL started just six days later.

THINK ABOUT IT

What sport would you want to play in college? Try to find out which colleges have the best teams or programs for that sport.

11
Number of NCAA Division I Men's Lacrosse Championships won by Syracuse University

- Syracuse has won the most men's LAX championships. Johns Hopkins has won nine. UVA has won six.
- Other top programs include Yale, Duke, Denver, and North Carolina.
- Maryland is the top NCAA Division I Women's school, with 14 championships.

Syracuse University has a top LAX program.

17

8

A Chance at the Pros

Many people love to play lacrosse. Only a few get the chance to go pro. There are just two outdoor men's leagues and one women's league. Open spots are limited.

Each pro league hosts an annual draft. Teams take turns choosing players. In 2019, the PLL drafted just 24 players. The MLL drafted 63 players. The WPLL drafted 25 new players for their five teams. Draftees come from colleges and universities.

The drafts are sometimes streamed online. Fans watch and wait to see which teams their favorite players will join. It is an exciting process. Leagues also host extra drafts. These aren't usually streamed. The teams choose players who have already graduated from college. They also choose international players

Only very top players get drafted into the pros each year.

in the extra drafts. Slowly but surely, they build their teams.

If players aren't drafted, they might still have a chance. Some pro teams offer open tryouts. Players can register, show up, and perform. If they impress the coaches, they might get a spot.

Some players go pro in other countries. They might play in an international league. They might play for a national team. Midfielder Jean-Luc Chetner played for Israel in the 2018 FIL World Lacrosse Championship. His father was born there. This was Chetner's first time traveling outside North America.

THINK ABOUT IT

If you could play sports in another country, where would you want to go?

2
Number of continents where defenseman Callum Robinson has played pro lacrosse

- Robinson played college lacrosse in the United States. Then he traveled to Australia to play in a pro league there.
- Since he was born in Australia, Robinson also played for their national team. His nickname is the "Big Koala."
- Robinson played in the MLL. Now he's a member of the PLL Blaze team.

9

Train Like a Pro

Lacrosse is a very physical game. Players must be fast. They run up and down the field during the game. The best players are the first to reach the net.

Overall fitness is important if you want to go pro. Distance running won't help a LAX athlete much. On the field, players run in short bursts. They also pass and shoot. They change direction very quickly. This makes agility a top concern. There are special drills and exercises that help increase agility.

The women's lacrosse team at Penn State does agility drills all summer. It helps them prepare for the season. They do quick sprints, hops, and shuffles. These drills help them develop fast footwork.

Michele DeJuliis was a standout on the Penn State team. She founded the Women's Professional Lacrosse League. She also runs a group called Ultimate Lacrosse. Players at her Ultimate camps learn kickboxing. This helps them build hand-eye coordination. They do strength training to help prevent injuries. They also receive training in confidence. This is often an overlooked skill on the LAX field.

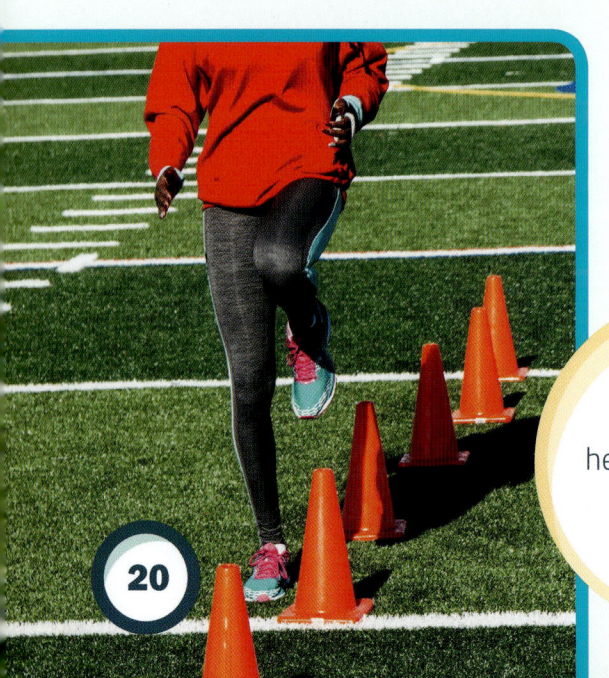

Agility drills help develop fast footwork on the field.

2011

Year when Kevin Crowley became the first LAX player to be selected No. 1 in two pro drafts

- Crowley doesn't just train during the off-season. He splits his year in two, playing in both the MLL and NLL.
- Box lacrosse helps Crowley prepare for his outdoor season, and vice-versa.
- Crowley is still the all-time points leader at Stony Brook University, scoring 232 points in four years.

Strong lacrosse players practice often. The team at Loyola University Maryland practices five days a week. They practice in the summer, too. They grow stronger and faster. For Loyola, the work is worth it. They ended 2019 as champions.

NLL player Kevin Crowley in 2015.

10

Safety and Equipment

Lacrosse is a contact sport. Players get hit with equipment and bodies. To prevent injury, they need the right gear.

Male athletes wear helmets with full face masks. A separate piece protects their teeth. They also wear gloves and shoulder pads. Some wear extra arm and rib pads, too. In addition to the regular equipment, the goalkeeper wears protectors for his throat and chest.

Women's lacrosse has less legal hitting. Female players wear goggles and mouthpieces, but no helmet or shoulder pads. Female goalkeepers wear helmets, padded gloves, chest protectors, and throat protectors. Both male and female players carry the crosse, or lacrosse stick. These come in a variety of lengths.

The LAX ball is made of solid rubber. When it flies at your body, it can pack a punch. Midfielders Kyle Hartzell

22

and Paul Rabil are tied for fastest lacrosse shot ever. They both shot a ball at 111 miles per hour (178 km/hr). Running and checking can cause injuries, too. The most common lacrosse injuries are strains and sprains.

Goalkeepers need extra protective equipment.

6
Number of teams in the Professional Lacrosse League, the newest pro league

- Players in the PLL wear shirts, shorts, and helmets featuring their teams' logos.
- Teams include the Whipsnakes, Redwoods, Chrome, Chaos, Atlas, and Archers.
- In 2019, the PLL struck a huge uniform deal with Adidas. It's the biggest such deal in pro lacrosse history.

A MENTAL GAME

LAX players must be physically fit. They also need to be mentally tough. Many coaches want their players to have high "lacrosse IQs." This means having a deep mental understanding of the game. It helps them play better and stay safe. Players can learn about lacrosse strategy. They can watch recordings of games. These things will help improve their lacrosse IQ.

11

Play Like a Champion

It's one thing to make it to the pros. It's an even greater achievement to get to the pro playoffs and championship. At the end of the pro lacrosse season, the top teams battle it out. The team that wins the playoffs is the champion.

In the MLL, four teams compete in the playoffs. Then two go head-to-head. The winning team gets the Steinfeld Trophy. It is named after the founder of the MLL, Jake Steinfeld. The Chesapeake Bayhawks have won the trophy five times. That's the most in MLL history.

The PLL has its own playoffs and championship. The WPLL holds a championship game in July. The New England Command won the

The Chesapeake Bayhawks have won the MLL Steinfeld Trophy five times.

24

A bronze Native American statue is in front of the National Lacrosse Hall of Fame.

6
Number of times John Grant Jr. has been on an MLL championship team

- Grant played with three pro leagues during his more than 20-year career. He played for the MLL, NLL, and Ontario Lacrosse Association.
- He also played in several indoor and outdoor world championships with the Canadian teams.
- In 2019, Grant announced he was coming out of retirement. At age 44, he will join the MLL's Denver Outlaws.

HALL OF FAMERS

The National Lacrosse Hall of Fame is in Sparks, Maryland. The Hall of Fame honors coaches, players, and other LAX greats. Over 400 people have been inducted since 1957. They are chosen by a voting process. Forward Ryan Boyle was recently inducted after an 11-year pro career in the MLL.

WPLL's first final in 2018. The team was down for most of the game. But coach Amy Patton had a feeling they would turn it around. When the confetti came down, the New England players had triumphed. They were the champs.

12

Giving Back

Pro lacrosse players don't make much money. Most have other full-time jobs. But the pro leagues still find ways to give back. They help local communities and groups in need. In 2017, the American Cancer Society was named the first official charity of the MLL. Teams in the MLL also hold gear auctions and theme games. These help raise funds for other partner charities.

The PLL has several charity initiatives. One supports US veterans. Veterans can get free game tickets. Players meet with them, too. The PLL also partners with the Headstrong Foundation to fight against cancer. A third program brings the game to kids who might not have access to teams and equipment.

Giving back isn't just about money. Players on the Boston Cannons MLL team go out of their way to give their time. They stay late after games to sign autographs, take selfies, and answer fan questions. They do this even when they are tired. They do this when they have lost. They want to inspire the next generation of LAX pros.

Scott Ratliff of the Atlanta Blaze promoting the American Cancer Society's Real Men Wear Pink Challenge in 2018.

2
Number of pro lacrosse players who started the Give & Go Foundation

- Adam Ghitelman and Scott Ratliff were inspired to start the organization after traveling together in 2014.
- The foundation seeks to spread LAX across the globe. They provide gear, coaching, and playing opportunities.
- Several other pros, including WPLL attacker Alex Aust, work with the foundation.

THINK ABOUT IT
If you ran a pro lacrosse team, would you partner with charities? What causes would you support?

The PLL supports US veterans and Wounded Warrior Sports Camps.

Fun Facts about Lacrosse

- The very first recorded game of women's lacrosse was played in 1890. It took place in Scotland at a school named St. Leonard's. The headmistress of the school brought the game from New Hampshire. On a visit there, she saw the game played between a Native American tribe and athletes from Montreal.

- For those who want to play lacrosse after college but don't go pro, there's another option. Across the United States and Canada, you can find hundreds of club teams. These teams are made up of adults who are past college age. They have their own local and regional leagues and tournaments.

There are lots of opportunities to play on club teams instead of going pro.

- Lacrosse fields used to be crowded. In early versions of the game, there could be up to 100 or 120 people on the field at once.

- Some Native American legends tell a story of lacrosse played by animals and birds. The Owl closely watched the ball. The Hawk and Eagle flew fast. The Great Turtle withstood hard hits. The Deer had agility and the Bear had his massive size. The story teaches a lesson about everyone having positive qualities, no matter their size.

- The first lacrosse sticks, used by Native tribes, were made of bent wood, leather, and animal products. These materials remained until the 1970s. That's when the plastic head was invented. It was attached to a wooden stick. In the 1980s, aluminum lacrosse sticks gained popularity. Today sticks are made from lightweight composites, with mesh pockets.

- Lacrosse is not an Olympic sport, but it could be one day. In 2018, the International Olympic Committee (IOC) "recognized" the Federation of International Lacrosse. This is the first step toward becoming an Olympic sport. Fans are excited. But there is still a long way to go.

Glossary

agility
The ability to move quickly, easily, and gracefully.

attacker
The offensive player whose job it is to score.

check
To hit an opponent with your body or lacrosse stick.

competitive
Situations in which some people are trying hard to be better or more successful than others.

crosse
A stick used to play lacrosse.

defender
In a game of lacrosse, a player who helps the goalkeeper protect the goal.

draft
The formal process of choosing players for sports teams.

face-off
In lacrosse, a battle to see which team will get possession of the ball. Face-offs occur at the beginning of the game, after halftime, and after each goal.

foam rolling
A type of exercise that uses a tube of compressed foam.

induct
To officially make someone a member of a group or club.

midfielder
A lacrosse athlete who plays across the entire field.

playoffs
Competitions played after the regular season has ended. The playoffs determine the league champion.

Read More

Bowker, Paul D. *Total Lacrosse.* Minneapolis, MN: SportsZone, 2017.

Braun, Eric. *Incredible Sports Trivia: Fun Facts and Quizzes.* Minneapolis, MN: Lerner Publishing Group, 2018.

Doeden, Matt. *More Than a Game: Race, Gender, and Politics in Sports.* Minneapolis, MN: Millbrook Press, 2020.

Myers, Jess. *Make Me the Best Lacrosse Player.* Minneapolis, MN: Abdo, 2017.

Visit 12StoryLibrary.com

Scan the code or use your school's login at **12StoryLibrary.com** for recent updates about this topic and a full digital version of this book. Enjoy free access to:

- Digital ebook
- Breaking news updates
- Live content feeds
- Videos, interactive maps, and graphics
- Additional web resources

Note to educators: Visit 12StoryLibrary.com/register to sign up for free premium website access. Enjoy live content plus a full digital version of every 12-Story Library book you own for every student at your school.

Index

championships, 5, 16-17, 24-25
charities, 26-27
college teams, 4, 8, 12, 16-17, 18
Crowley, Kevin, 21

daily life, 5, 6
draft, 18-19, 30

equipment, 22-23

Federation of International Lacrosse, 5, 29

Grant, John Jr., 25

Harrison, Kyle, 7
history, 8-9

injuries, 20, 22-23

Jones, Myles, 15

leagues, 4, 10-11, 13, 18-19, 23, 28

mental fitness, 23

National Lacrosse Hall of Fame, 25
Native Americans, 8-9, 25, 28-29

Rabil, Paul, 7, 23
Ratliffe, Scott, 6, 26-27
Robinson, Callum, 19
rules, 9, 11, 13

salaries, 4, 6, 11
Sweeney, Kyle, 5

Thompson brothers, 8
training, 6, 20

women's teams, 12-13

youth teams, 14-15

About the Author

Kaitlyn Duling has written over 60 books for children and teens. She loves to learn about sports. Kaitlyn lives in Washington, DC, where she roots for the University of Maryland lacrosse teams.

READ MORE FROM 12-STORY LIBRARY

Every 12-Story Library Book is available in many fomats. For more information, visit **12StoryLibrary.com**